THE unbearable HEART

THE
unbearable
HEART

For Barry,
Best wishes and thank
you for your words,
comments, photos, presence
in our evening anxiety
ann —

KIMIKO HAHN *Kimiko Hahn*

12/95

KAYA PRODUCTION
1995

Published by KAYA PRODUCTION, NEW YORK

©1995 BY KIMIKO HAHN

Page **67** serves as an extension to this copyright page.

Paperback ISBN **1-885030-01-0**

Cloth ISBN **1-885030-00-2**

Library of Congress Catalogue Number **94-75769**

Printed and Bound in the United States of America

Book Design by **YUKO UCHIKAWA/MAKERS'STUDIO**

"... when is closure an ending?"
— Melvin Dixon

FOR

MY SISTER

TOMIE

AND

MY DAUGHTERS

MIYAKO

AND REIKO

Love to **TED HANNAN** "without whom."

A heartfelt thanks to **WALTER LEW** for his *premonitions.*

The author also thanks the fellowship programs at the **NATIONAL ENDOWMENT FOR THE ARTS** and the **NEW YORK FOUNDATION FOR THE ARTS** for their generous support. Some of these poems have appeared in the **AMERICAN VOICE, ASIAN PACIFIC AMERICAN JOURNAL, BOMB, HANGING LOOSE, IKON, MĀNOA, MUÆ, PENNSYLVANIA REVIEW, POETRY FLASH, PREMONITIONS: THE KAYA ANTHOLOGY OF NEW ASIAN NORTH AMERICAN POETRY.**

Cover contact sheet by **WALTER HAHN**, 1956.

CONTENTS

THE
TOLL
ATTENDANT

whiter under a fluorescent halo
horn-rimmed and high-pitched
collects our coins and gives directions
to the hospital where mother's body
may be retrieved at our earliest convenience,
to a land perpetually 3:20 am
rain always raining heavily
and to where her two daughters and two sons-in-law
travel in the family station wagon
to tell father mother is gone.
The toll attendant points beyond the plaza lights
into the dark that will become the hospital.
And when we reach the emergency room father smiles
glad someone will finally assure him
Maude is all right.

In the train an hour along the Sound, distant from the details of grief
I look up from the news toward the salt marshes
clumped beneath a snow we thought we would not see this year;
snow fallen twice this past week since mother died, instantly, 10:35 pm,
broadsided by an Arab kid fleeing a car of white kids with baseball bats;
a snow only matched by my father's head as I reach to touch him
as I have never touched him. He wishes
he could see her once more, to say goodbye,
as Ted and I said goodbye to the body that was mother's.
Grief comes in spasms: the smell of banana bread, I think of the rotting fruit
my sister and I tossed before father came home from Yonkers General.
A flashlight. The flashlight she bought my youngest daughter
who always rummaged for one under grandpa's side of the mattress.
The orange day lilies the florist sent to our apartment:
the lilies from the woods she brought to my wedding.

And after I told my six-year-old, grandma died in the accident,
after tears and questions she suggested, maybe now is a good time
to explain what the man has to do with babies.
So I chose one perfect lily from that vase
and with the tip of a paring knife slit open the pistil
to trace the passage pollen makes to the egg cell—
the eggs I then slipped out and dotted on her fingertip, their greenish-white
translucent as the air in this blizzard that cannot cool the unbearable heart.

As I write this, I still demand your attention, mother.

And now that she's gone how do we find her—
especially my small daughters who will eventually recall their grandmother
not as a snapshot in the faults of the mind
but as the incense in their hair long after the reading of the Lotus Sutra.

THE
STRAY

Father, Tomie and I stand at the hospital window
to look beyond our lives without mother
and see a stray calico dart into rubbish.
There is something there it wants.

THE
RIVER AND
THE LIGHTS

I cannot see the river as I drive along it
nor the bridge though its sharp lights
pierce through the humid air.
The flowering cherry and apple trees
appear as phantoms wafting in the night
under the yellow lamps.
I drive away from the funeral arrangements,
from the constant scent of mother in each corner
of every box and basket my father rummages through.
Even outside buying a newspaper he pauses at the jeweler's
noting what would become her.
Or weeding the lawn he expects her to kneel beside him
in the crabgrass. The air outside distracts me.
It is thick as the incense
that will saturate our hair and best clothes
as we listen to the Lotus Sutra
an incantation recited for thousands of years.
I could drive on this parkway for hours
but I am here under the anxious restaurant signs of Manhattan
where I am the mother of two daughters
as my mother was the mother of two daughters.
I must park, climb the stairs and turn the key to my floor-through,
a light on in every room.

for father

A CIRCLE
OF LANTERNS

Walking through a light rain
that quenches even the pavement
we turn from the funeral service
toward a Chinese banquet where
we will eat tofu, rice and vegetables
prepared in seven different ways.
En route my older child asks
why grandma's body was not at the temple
and I am cornered by her need for reasons:

"Because grandma wished to be cremated.
After death the body can't feel anything—"
"Like hair?"
"Yes, like hair. So the body
is placed in a special fire
that releases the spirit, leaving only ashes.
Grandma's ashes are in a box at the temple."
She is silent, then:
"Some people say dead people are reborn."
"Some people believe that. I believe
grandma is now wind, sunlight and moonlight."
She adds after dinner, "And mist."

The reverend explains that the Bon Festival this July
will be our mother's hatsu bon: the first time
we dress in kimono, pin up our hair and rouge our cheeks
to dance under the circle of lanterns for her
as she taught me in Kahului when I was four.
When I was ready to learn everything.

THE
FRAGRANCE

Father says he would do anything to retrieve her—
the kind of bargain in folk tales where the Sweet Beauty
is returned in exchange for a famine that razes the countryside.
And yet, what hell is this where each article
emits the fragrance of mother's cold cream.

FOUR WEEKS AFTER MOTHER'S FUNERAL

my sister tells me she has sat on pillows
and wept all day
giving me a kind of permission
to weep without stopping for what seems hours;
my body shakes,
I cannot catch my breath.
Ted circles his palm on my back
as if polishing wood.
After I collapse into sleep
our youngest daughter cries out from her bed
to tell us of a nightmare she cannot recall.

FORECAST

Since mother's death the ceiling settles
close to the trees, the buds,
a texture of red haze over the hills along the parkway.
Now mist. Now a cloud burst.
Even without sun the cherries lining the river
in one night it seems, blossom.
How they can I do not know.

THE
IRIS

Since the PATCO Strike
I think of death days before a flight
and today as I coordinate babysitters,
chart outfits and menus I also think
of your mother six months preparing her bulky husband
and distributing her sweaters and bracelets
as medicine could not contain her breast cancer.
All the advice. The affection placed
so consciously. The greeting of an absolute.
I imagine you watching her clip the stems off flowers
under the faucet, dropping an aspirin in the vase.
Were they iris?

For C

FOR
MY ONCE MOTHER-IN-LAW,
FOR ASAYE

This holiday, dishes piled in the sink,
turkey gutted and wrapped, stuffing
consumed, a few pie slices on the counter,
my sister wipes the table and father
brings out mother's jewelry. We've put off
dividing these years of gifts for eight months
since mother's sudden death;
now father twitches to have these boxes
out of his constant sight. My sister wants it over.
I'd delay this meeting longer—block
the surprise when we open a little box,
the handling of each piece, the desire for a particular one
mixed with childhood rivalry and
adoration. Recalling the silver bells from India
she wore with a yellow tent dress. The red coral
against a black sweater. The Tibetan donkey
my daughters chewed in their infancies.
The black dog that resembles Felix the Cat—a folksy netsuke
that catches my breath each time I unfold its tissue.
Where did father purchase it—Mitsukoshi, 1965?
And here is a delicate snow pea,
a milky translucent jade my father noticed
before his train left Shanghai. It is this fragile pod
I ask you to take, Asaye,
who was once my mother-in-law, whom
I have loved since I was, what? twelve?
And whose oldest son, not my husband now,

was my beloved in those brisk years of becoming
a woman. Would you take this and someday
pass it along to your new daughter-in-law?
An odd passage. But who knows how this jade
came to the artisan's block and blade:
Which mountain did the stone cutter climb?
from what vein was it mined? how thick
was the mist in the valley when he surfaced?
—stone finally polished in a humid village I can imagine
but barely pronounce.

THE
SWIMMER'S
BLOOD

We survive recalling crests just off the shore
beyond the children's bobbing games
but before the swimmer, the elderly woman
in a skirted aqua swimsuit and rubber bathing cap.
She dove over the waves and now swims
slowly in the post-storm turbulence
hand-over-hand, feet splashing evenly,
her head turning in measures of breath.
The waves roll her up. She must be around 75, the age
of my mother-in-law before years of cigarettes
destroyed her internal organs.
I imagine seeing Anne with such a casual stroke
against undertow and current. It may not have mattered
after settling the girls into solid schools
that I don't play cribbage, that I don't
swim comfortably in such depth,
that my maternal grandparents were peasants from Hiroshima.
In those early immigrant years
grandfather was lucky to find a wife
among the farm families already on Maui
while his friends flipped through pictures and astrology charts.
From a single photo I know Mitsuye was delicate
with strong eyebrows that suggest a playfulness
that would save her as she labored first
to put her brothers and sisters through professional schools
then raise eight squabbling children (squabbling still);
she was lucky not to be misled by rumors and refinished photos

to find Katsunosuke, a man under 25 and handsome.
I wonder if he had the energy after plantation work
to be kind to her: not merely sexual but comforting.
And I am fortunate to watch this woman swim
what would equal laps in a pool and thank Anne
for the swimmer's blood in my daughters' skinny frames
darting in and out of the surf
competing with each other for who will swim out
with their father first
beyond the swathes of seaweed into the Atlantic.

for V

THE
FLOODING

The girls have disgruntled themselves to sleep
as father drives us home in the rain
after the first holiday dinner since mother's death.
We speak without looking. I begin:

I write about mother all the time.
I can't stop myself. I have a new piece
in which I use lines from sympathy notes—
   If you need more I must have a hundred—
   Look at this bend, how the water floods.
I have enough.
   See how they dug out a pond for the drain-off—
I was tired of fragmenting the text
as in my last collection. I wanted something
with no disruption; without
references to Genji. Another obsession—
   I haven't seen such a downpour in a while,
   go on.
But in an early draft I knew
I would return to Genji's relationships
and explore his own quick death.
   Well after all any poem for mother
   would be a love poem—
True.
   Look how the road slants, see it?
   the pools along the left shoulder?
I never noticed before.
The text is a collage of Genji references

and the sympathy notes—
      A collage—like my collages—
      surprisingly difficult
      to paint a good picture then
      tear it up, destroy any figurative aspect.
Exactly. Only mine is a collage of lines
on not being able to speak.
That there are no words—
      Yes—
For me there must be a way to articulate—
      Here's another bad area.
So the Genji material is also
on bereavement. How to grieve. Express loss—
      Especially since he himself died midway—
becomes a model for his own children.
      Remember I have an anthology I bought years ago:
      Japanese death poems—though not all written
      on the death bed. The samurai ones—
the classic cherry blossom—
      Right. Borrow it if you'd like.
So I've decided to take my obsessions farther—
fragment the narrative, disrupt the text
every time the reader engages.
Create a language of disruption. Begin a line,
sever it. Begin again, interrupt.
At times with a single word: BEAR! LILY! whatever.
I'm pleased with the poem so far. It's long.
      Oh, did I tell you about the tv show on seers?
      where the producer tried to trick this man who
      is quite well known for speaking to those
      who have died? He began seeing figures

when he was seven right after the mumps.
Strange. They couldn't trick him.
Which means he can either speak to the dead
or read the minds of people before him.
Give them incredible details of their loved ones.
Memories.

Like Susan.

Yes, her sensing mother's presence haunts me—
but positively. I wish—

I even feel envious.

Well, it wouldn't be you or me. We're—

too in control.

Yes. Too in control.

Yes.

Here's where the accident, where they say
the accident was. I can't distinguish between
what may be a memory or what the officers
told me—was it only eight months ago?

Yes.

I've been driving this route for twenty years,
know the tilt of the road, the poor drainage,
where the flooding will be—
and try to drive around it. Especially
in such a downpour as tonight.
I would love to see the poem. Ah!

WISTERIA

Speech is always a problem, learning
goodbye means bye, bye,
something-something-alligator—defying the verb to be.
A wave. A disappearance: the latch, the back
of father's pea jacket, the car engine.
Leaving for the university.
But even as a crisis of articulation
there were words when a car broadsided mother's car
and killed her instantly ten months ago.
Even as the noise of weeping. Even
as sympathy notes express:

>   *there are no words*
>   *what can one say*
>   *if there were words*

because there are always words. Just as

                         BEAR

            LILY

                                    ORBIT

are words for the nouns we count on.
Genji knew this as he rose
through the dank sorrow of Fujitsubo's death:
the beauty who, he was told, resembled
the mother who died in his childhood;
the woman he adored, courted, who was his stepmother,
who gave birth to his child though all the world
believed Kaoru, "fragrance,"
to be the Emperor's, his father.

She was mother. Later nun. Then dead. Then

                    HEART
    SILK
          SNOW

The exquisite instrument to find his mother.
The stunning search, unfulfilled. Treacherous.

          QUILT

Treacherous quilt. Elegant confusion. Aesthetic metamorphosis.

What happens when the emblem of
one's need, then the surrogate of the emblem
passes away, is lost—
"Father, we have lost mother."

          QUILT

He found words when nothing else in the world
served him. Not his legitimate or illegitimate children.
His wives or lovers. Not the countless women
he took in dark corridors
some as young as his daughter, one,
his daughter through adoption. Many as if raped.
Objectives. Objecting. Objects of his heart. Stand-ins for
all the nights he could not have any mother.

          RIVER

He collected articles such as a fan from Yugao
and the mementos comforted even as they provoked.
He found these tools enabled his heart
to climb, as wisteria. To confound
                    what is unutterable
                        words seem inadequate
                            impossible to say
to outdistance denotation
                            impossible to say anything of use
                        no words of consolation
                    will explain when I see you
He became a model of grief. A person
for whom words were a stunning means for

     FISH

for the rise of reparation. Messages
delivered to a distant room. Sought outside court.
Carried to a mountain retreat.
Even though Genji himself died halfway through the novel
I am not finished with him
just as other characters were not finished
with him or his contagious heart

     SALT

or naturally their own narratives,
solely, collectively. Linear
or spatial. Always a shared constellation.
Narratives interdependent as an economy.

CUP

HOT WATER

■■■

Leaving a bunraku performance on West 57th Street,
how many red lights or corners did my parents encounter
before the moment one car intercepted another
and the medical team lay mother's body, already dead,
on the road in the rain to attempt resuscitation.
The last to touch her: doctor, mortician, crematorium attendant.
Goodbye. In the wet road, on the stretcher, *goodbye.*
In the furnace, *goodbye.*
This narrative will not leave the boy who was racing traffic lights
because words permeate the unconscious.
Because I will not stop.
   if there were anything I could say

■■■

A friend who lost her mother to breast cancer calls.
Lost. As if one could find her
wandering in a forest. Or swimming beyond the coral reef
hair trailing like a mermaid.
Or in a monastery to avoid some one or thing—
loss, sharp as the pricks we call stars
although sometimes we mistake a planet for that celestial moment.

  MOON

 SATELLITE

Then there was the Moon maiden a woodcutter found
shining in a bamboo stalk; the infant he brought to his barren wife.
Did you mourn when she returned to that scarred surface?
Would Genji have read such a tale to Murasaki?
to make her fear loss? to make her obey?
distrust her own stupid papa?

SNOW

No, not SNOW
If there were words for the place in the body

SPARROW

that cannot stop convulsing when twilight
turns everything gray and noiseless

SPARROW

even the tidy poems, immaculate and imperial,
Genji fashioned for the one he could not possess
just as he could not possess his mother's breast—
the poems would only circle his desire.

CAT

We may call this business our *gut*
rather than heart which is a muscle
and not as central as some other organ.
We may call this narrative *mouth* because we cry so loudly
the neighbor's baby wakes and cries also.

So loudly it feels good.

The author was not finished with Genji
just as I am not finished with mother
though I still will not talk to her—
                you will talk to her as if
though I have sat by the sea to shout, *come back.*
To me.
If only I could believe in the metaphysical world
I discover amidst utensils.

SCISSORS

In belief systems.   ·

SQUAWROOT

Though of course language ceases
just as dreaming or waking may blur but are separate.

FEVER

TEMPERATURE

I want to hold on to what is not tangible, I know.
The ashes. The air.
To the sun after weeks of rain
drying the apartment's humid floor and odor,
the slickness, the paperback book covers that roll
like discarded scrolls. To see the cloud
descended on the dunes burnt off. The mist evaporated.

■■■

The seven-year-old wishing she could die
so she might see her again
at least understands grandmother will never return:
It's been too long since we've seen her. But what if
I jump from the window and change my mind—

■■■

WING

CRANE

TRUCK   FUCK

■■■

                    MILK

Nomination. Who teaches us the noises
we apply to the articles surrounding us,
that become more separate each day,
more false and willful and dead.

HAT

STROLLER

KEY CHAIN

When can we sit up, hold a spoon. Feed ourselves.
That dragonflies are not ravens.
That we cannot possess either of their abilities
to communicate.

I am not finished with Genji
just as I fear father will never cease becoming a model
for what I try to articulate.
Before he left the hospital and its "intensive care unit"
he asked me to write a poem for him.
It is a *waka*.
But I want to write another one
with the central metaphor, a boat.

Even as the other characters are not satisfied
they, too, become models of grief, for him,
for his own never-completed search.

Even as I disrupt the narrative to promote disruption,
even to disrupt the parent we learned from.

Before father visited for the first time without mother
our youngest daughter tells us she has
a house in her body and in this house is grandmother
and the goldfish and cat who have also died.

But most of the time words do not progress logically:

SHELL BENCH MOTHER BRUSH

And some astonish everyone:

WAVE

FIN

BOAT

CUTTINGS

a *zuihitsu* for father

My younger sister and I, cleaning father's house before he returns from a week in intensive care, rush to dispose of mother's cosmetics, store her jewelry for a later date, and phone a woman's shelter to pick up bags of dresses, size 4, and shoes, 4 1/2, even stopping to laugh at the platforms from "the mod era" she swore would come back. We collapse into each other's arms and cry *mommy mommy* as if she could hear us if we wept loud enough.

I look out the taxi window at everyone else's life. Certainly all the people in all the little apartments have gone about their business making money off other people's mortgages or addictions, without the knowledge my mother died last week, someone who found pleasure in baking oddly shaped biscuits with her granddaughters.

I keep my father talking about his boyhood—his passion for deep-sea diving though he grew up on Lake Michigan, his going AWOL for art courses, the four books at the Naval Library on "Oriental Art." Here we turn, always return, to Maude who *wasn't supposed to go first*. He said he had her convinced.

I ask Marie how to tell the girls, Miya now six and Rei, four. She advises we speak to them separately, to allow each their own reactions.

The funeral director says, "She doesn't look 68, but then oriental women never look their age." He then reminisces about "The War."

I want to throw out as much as possible—a half-jar of expensive cream, a suede jacket—belongings my sister wishes to hold on to. I go to the Funeral Home. I find comfort in The 10 O'clock News; she resents the superficial, even stupid resemblance of normality.

Two weeks now since mother died. Tuesday nights, I stay with father now a man who can barely contain what, in a second, became memory. He lurches from each small room testing himself against souvenirs: animal puppets from Rome, 1956; a Noh mask, Kyoto, '64; silver rabbit, Phnom Penh, '65; hotel towel, Chicago, '70. Even after discarding her dresses and middle-class perfumes she inhabits every corner of every project—collage, painting, carving. He recalls telling her when they first met at the Art Institute that art would always come before any thing and any one.

We toast Maude at a neighbor's, drinking what we like since she couldn't tolerate liquor. Janet remembers the day she knew they'd be friends: "We were looking at the peonies by the stone wall and your mother said, *Know what these remind me of? Penises.*" Our laughter resembles sobbing.

She reread stories as often as I demanded.

Convinced and convincing me through my early twenties I could not sew or cook despite home ec. classes and odd advice, she cooked and froze stews, checked if I ever baked potatoes and the last day we saw her, sent us home with turkey leftovers. It's true I've never roasted one.

The first thing I saw when I returned to clean their house were my three skirts, pinned and draped across the ironing board.

How suddenly grievances against father evaporate, steam rising from an icy river. He even corrects himself, calling mother, *a woman.*

Why is pain deeper than pleasure, though it is a pleasure to cry so loud the arthritic dog hobbles off the sunny carpet, so loud I do not hear the phone ring, so loud I feel a passion for mother I thought I reserved for lovers. I insert a CD and sing about a love abandoned, because there are no other lyrics for this.

Pulling off a crewneck sweater I bend my glasses and for the next few days wear the frames off-center not realizing the dizzy view is in fact physical.

Theresa, David, Liz, Mark, Sharon, Denise, Carmen, Sonia, Susan, Lee, Cheryl, Susan, Jo, John, Jerry, Doug, Earlene, Marie, Robbin, Jessica, Kiana, Patricia, Bob, Donna, Orinne, Shigemi—

Suddenly the tasks we put off need to get done: defrost the freezer, pay the preschool bill, order more checks.

For 49 days after her own mother's death she did not eat meat. I didn't know, mother. I'm sorry, I didn't know.

The sudden scent of her spills from her handbag—leather, lotion, mints, coins. I cannot stand.

She had marked April 28 to see Okinawan dancers.

He has not yet slept in their bed, because the couch in front of the television *feels firmer* to his seven broken ribs.

At dinner we play a story game; the youngest one asks, "about grandma?" then corrects herself quickly "about bunny rabbit" as she momentarily trips on her own preoccupation.

Father tells me there is a Japanese story about a mask maker who has a daughter renowned for her stunning beauty. Upon her untimely death, how he does not recall, the father sits by her side to sketch the exquisite features. Poetic license. Though mother did look beautiful I had never seen a face devoid of any expression, an aspect even a painting would somehow contain.

The children notice he has taken off his wedding ring.

At a favorite cafe I hear a newborn in the next booth wailing for, probably, the mother's breast, as if his life will end this second. It is my cry.

Shrimp. An image of my parents at a card table shelling shrimp the night before my sister's wedding, the peels translucent pink as my mother's finger-nails. Primitive and reassuring.

At the house in Paia where grandma washed other people's laundry and raised her chickens, and grandpa sat in his wheelchair, we had a toilet inside but also the old outhouse, a rickety two-seater. I would go in, close the gray-painted door, latch the hook and sit on the edge holding my breath against the frothy stench of shit. You could hear your waste hit bottom. The dim light lent privacy against peeping cousins.

She taught me to pluck or cut flowers near the roots for the long stems. Recut under water. She taught me to rub my finger and thumb together over the silver dollar sheath, to rub off the brown membrane and scatter the seeds on my skirt. Gently so as not to tear the silver inside. I see them and think of her name, not Maude, but Mother.

Father and I bring the ashes into the City and plan to drop them off at the temple. Mrs. K has Buddhist robes over her blue jeans and suggests she recite a sutra. We light incense in the half-light. I forget tissues. My face and sleeves are covered with tears and mucus. My shoulders shake silently as listening.

Three months have past. I count the days from March 10th to the 100th day for another memorial service.

lotus suture

As if a metaphor for mother's death the Rodney King verdict and rebellion in Los Angeles breaks open urban areas across the country. It is a complex set of issues where some Korean shops and whites are attacked as the emblems of the establishment. But what is the establishment? Why not the actual property relations? Who actually owns the buildings, makes the laws—I feel helpless. Embittered.

Cuttings she had placed in tumblers in the kitchen and bathroom offer their fragile roots.

Rei discusses mother's death with me. A babysitter told her not to talk about it. Another told her it is *like sleep*. I tell her to talk. I tell her it is not sleep although the person looks asleep but he or she will not wake. She wants to talk to grandma and asks if she can. I tell her if she wants to she can; then I ask her what she wants to say. She wants to tell her to wake up.

People who have died but were revived speak of a dark tunnel with a fierce light at the end. Is it a passage or is it the memory of birth?

Miya speaks of dying—to see grandma again. I am shocked and try to say something.

I can see her body, not *her*, her body lying in a pine box, hands folded, black and white hair combed back, the funeral home odor saturating the drapes and carpets of the respectfully lit parlors. I said goodbye but it was really *to myself*.

I wish I had snipped off a bit of hair. I recall the braid she kept for a while in her drawer.

I purchase an expensive "anti-wrinkle defense cream" at the discount pharmacy. The third morning my skin really feels smoother though the burgeoning lines have not faded. I think something I've only thought the night before the plane trip: will I live to see the bottom of this jar.

Miya has shelved her grief and when admonished she declares: everything was fine until grandma died.

For the first time father harvests a half-dozen bamboo shoots from a small grove on the side of the house. Mother had spoken of gathering them as a child in Hawaii, soaking then boiling then sizzling them. He finds a recipe and experiments. He sends some home with me. They taste like artichoke hearts. We all think of mother. And I think of a poem from the *Manyōshu* about a trowel.

He plays her lottery numbers.

The lawyer of the kid who broadsided their car sends a letter threatening to sue father if he does not respond in five days with information. We feel naive, in a state of disbelief at the vulgar tone of the letter.

I wear the silk pants she altered for me: a forgotten pin, sewn into the hem, sticks into my ankle.

At any moment of the day I can hear her admonishment: *oh, Kimi.* She especially disliked spills.

I do not want to write about her death. But I do not want to lose these strong feelings.

Rei does not stop chattering about her: We have no one to make slush. She always had gum in her handbag. She read to us in Japanese and knew "cat's cradle" backward.

The 100th Day Anniversary. The weather is already warm. Her brother from Honolulu tells about her letters to him during World War II when he was in the 442nd.

We vacation on Fire Island. A few deer walk by the porch so close we can see how fuzzy their antlers are.

I keep recalling the diagram of the accident scene. Mother's body lying on the highway where medics attempted CPR. I imagine the wet black road, the traffic signals changing despite the halt.

Christmas ornaments last packed away by her: the balls she and father decorated with cherubs and glitter, old wooden angels and soldiers from my childhood, tinsel carefully rewrapped.

Some days I have a thought to write down but let it go.

During a week-long visit to the snowy fields of Vermont, I hear of a car bomb explosion at the World Trade Center, killing and injuring many people. The world continues outside this quiet. And the death of those who happen to step in its ordinary traffic.

I stop writing altogether. And when I must—postcards, single lines after a commute—the writing ends with mother.

Afraid father is "seeing someone" and hopeful. I extend mother's jealousy into the afterlife. It becomes my own hell.

I begin to feel impatient with father over little things like whether my hair is trimmed evenly. I wonder if my annoyance indicates we are moving on.

Father finds an envelope of marigold seeds mother saved and lets the children scatter them. The composted earth smells fertile like the pail she kept with egg shells and melon rinds.

CRUISING BARTHES

1. "Many readings are perverse, implying a split, a cleavage. Just as the child knows its mother has no penis and simultaneously believes she has one..." [47]

I cannot recall believing my mother possessed
the same genitalia as father
though I've never seen, in memory, my parents naked.
The first penis I saw must have been a tiny one,
almost as miniscule as a woman's clitoris,
that part of her self my three-year-old calls her penis
ever since she showered with Ted or me
and noticed the reassuring differences
not as anxieties leading to envy
except perhaps for peeing in the park
and even then she can skillfully pee, standing up.
Not leading to envy because, she corrected me
after I corrected her,
girls have penises also.
And showed me hers as proof,
as if I might not know.
And though it isn't true she has a penis
she has what she's decidedly named a penis.
So Barthes' metaphor is inexact.
His split, the site of loss and bliss
cannot be illustrated by a dated interpretation
though shapes can indicate aspects of memory or vision.
I prefer thinking of this split
as the mother's labia parting for conception,
stretching, even tearing for birth and afterbirth.
I'd rather imagine the lover's tongue
there. The husband's swollen cock
compelled to reach the uterus and coming as close as cervix.

Here is the site where a severe emotion can unfold
not unlike the graphite of a draft when the mesmerized
fist narrates faster than the brain.
I do not want a penis, dear Freud, or even mother's breast,
dear Klein. I want to tunnel
away from light to half-light,
from the sounds that articulate our loss finally,
the most primitive irony,
where what *is* simultaneous is not the noun cleavage
but the verb, *cleave*: to split
or to cling. That pleasure.

2. "Thus the Biblical myth is reversed, the confusion of tongues is no longer a punishment, the subject gains access to bliss by the cohabitation of languages *working side by side*: the text of pleasure is a sanctioned Babel." [4]

The way I imagine a baby first comes to hear
the cadence of his/her mother's language in utero,
the way one lies in a dim wallpapered room
and hears someone running the bath water,
hears it deepening to bass, the way
Williams determined his meter listening to voices from another room,
or I listened to mother read the tale of Urashimataro
who rode a tortoise down through plankton
to a sea kingdom, able to breathe under water,
to speak to animals, the way I understood
the story though she read it in Japanese
and translated later so I could compare my version
from sound and pictures to the original;
the way *tsunami* has entered the English language,
pain, from the Portuguese, has entered Japanese: *pan*.
The way father would not believe mother died
when a kid's car broadsided his.

The way my husband's mother would not accept his collect call
from the hospital when our daughter was born.
The way I love my husband and, too, the possibility
of taking a lover: positioning him behind me
to wrap his arms around my breasts, his mouth on my neck
the inside of my head faint. The way I write about
the possibility crazing the surface,
the body fluids, diffusing
the relationship of nonfiction to fiction.
The way I fear speaking Japanese and adore
speaking it. The way I teach my daughters Japanese
through song: *yamano oterano kanega naru.*
The way Heian women overpowered the culture so I would
someday, hundreds of years and half a globe away
at a "post-feminist" point of departure
recite from their pulse: *sasou mizu araba*—
the way I write this line of Ono no Komachi with a ball point.
The way I do not punish myself.

3. **intellectual solidarities, political assertion, the dissolve, plausible
neologisms, abrasions, image-reservoirs, image systems, language-substance**

I have fallen into a state of desire
for the author who can manipulate such language
as if fording a river he has known since boyhood.
I need him. He is, as he suggests of others,
the hypostatized father we write about
when we write about anything: hat, cherry tree,
monopoly capitalism. These are the worlds
from which I recover the sense of learning words
for the first time, when mother
pointed to a ball and said *ball,*
when father entered the room

and I said *dada*. And since mother
died in a car crash three months ago
the men have turned into mother,
parts of her, parts of her speech:
Kimi's bottle. And I begin to learn
not so much about loss,
because I began to learn about that
when my sister was born
but how to continue, a text, a desire,
resume the process of narration.
That water. That current. That mouth.

4. "The professor is someone who finishes his sentences." [50]

5. "What can't be used for sustenance is fashioned into toys." [*LIFE* JUNE '92, PAGE 56]

6. "Bringing itself to the limits of speech, in a *mathesis* of language which does not seek to be identified with science, the text undoes nomination, and it is this defection which approaches bliss." [45]

I play the fringes of clarity
so *word* and *world* confuse the typesetter's fingers, so *he* and *she*
are only a letter apart and the narrative
skips over the brain as it is written from heart
to keyboard. The story of my grandmother
appears on the monitor:
Kimichan, try eat melicanguaba, ne. Is that Japanese?
Is it Japanese? Am I Japanese?
Are you Japanese, Grandma?
Mother intervenes:
Mama, it's American: American-guava.
But what is my answer?

What is Japanese? blood,
geography, translations by white, Occupation-trained
academic men? I am four.
I am in Hawaii visiting my grandparents.
My mother is pregnant though I do not know it yet.
I love words. I love to watch my grandmother wash dishes
in water so hot steam rises from
her hands after she closes the faucet.
The story on the monitor is yellow.
There are a set of facts I can adjust
around a child and her grandmother's confusion.
I can always feel that confusion
and forever be angry
or fall in love with the ambiguity
that allows the typist to type without thought.

7. Rumbek was twelve in the spring of 1989 hoeing his father's field in the southern Sudan when horsemen razed his village. After dark he found his brother, Tabor, and wandered through the bush for three months. They reached a camp of 9,000 boys. They heard their parents had been slaughtered. Their sister perhaps sold. Before then, fifteen of their band died by not cooking a cassaba correctly. They had to leave the poisoned bodies. Several were caught by hyenas while the others could only climb trees and wait till the animals finished. A hundred drown fording a river. Life in the camps consists of searching for food—edible leaves and roots, fruits, small animals. There is no trash: what is not used for sustenance is reworked into toys. Older children adopt younger ones. When there are classes the ones who attend while others forage recite the lessons at night. Here the English word *bottle* may become mispronounced, *boskle*. Someday you may retell this narrative if only as a flash in your mind while showering.

8. "discomfort"

Real bliss, if acknowledged, is not in the routine
that bludgeons passion but yes, in disturbance:
that razor stubble chaffing labia, that scent
from every fold or hollow.
The lover you must meet in an office.
Unveiled. Disrobed. Not even in love.
He thought he might be, she wished she were
until he really did leave for Ann Arbor.
And she washed in the lavatory down the corridor
while considering software.

9. It is odd that some words for beautiful objects sound nauseating,
such as *magnolia*, unlike the lovely *night soil*.

10. "The boys devise crude writing implements and scavenge for school
supplies as they do for food." [*LIFE* JUNE '92, PAGE 55]

11. While the father shaves at the sink his two-year-old looks at his
penis, points to the circumcised tip and says, *hat*.

12. "...what [writing aloud] searches for (in a perspective of bliss) are the
pulsional incidents..."[66-7]

The bliss within the pulsional incidents
of articulation must actually be experienced in utero:
maternal heartbeat or gait, fetal hiccoughs,
and inflections conducted through liquid and tissue.
At times there is music. Other times
a sibling drums passionately. The radical throbbing
of labor itself of course. I don't know
when memory begins though I quiz my daughter

against early possibilities:
a mobile of penguins, a set of pastel paints.
But perhaps such early recollections
do not reside in images
but in an ambiguity closer to
the physical memory of a wound or ache.

In a room full of couples and paintings I curl up on a couch
and place my fingers on my infant's pulsing fontanel
my hand that close to the unconscious.

The Crab

Good thing my daughter is clever
as my husband is stupid. In the market last week
she took pity on a crab about to be speared,
bought it and let it go by the bay.
Some way to spend your money,
but it's your business, I told her.
That same day as my husband was hoeing
he saw a snake about to devour a frog.
He tried to stop it by pulling the frog back
with the tip of the hoe
but it was already half inside the snake's mouth.
Out of compassion he cried: Snake,
let it go and I'll give you my daughter.
To his surprise, the snake disgorged the green thing
and slithered off.
That night a gentleman came for our daughter.
My husband managed to gain a night
before he took her forever.
Meanwhile my daughter discovered his idiotic pledge
and hid in our chest.
The next night the snake returned as a snake
slunk under the door and banged on the chest
with its hefty tail.
Help me please! our daughter cried
but it seemed her fate was sealed.
Just then a small image of Kannon appeared
telling her not to worry.
Soon, a hundred crabs
crawling through every window and crack
tore the snake into shreds and left.
I turned back to my cooking.

The Fan

Walking along Suzaku Avenue I met a woman
as ravishing as the twilight
over dark winter branches,
as those orange clouds, as the breeze
lifting dust by my geta.
I needed her and told her she equalled the Sun Goddess
in complexion and character.
She smiled faintly in the dusk,
her red lips juicy as I imagined her sex
and soon we were off hand-in-hand
down a back street to her room.
As I began to unwrap the silks off her breasts and hips
taste the buds of her nipples,
she told me we couldn't make love ever
or I would die. *Crazy woman, prick tease*, I thought
and the fire under my skin burned off my clothes
till I was at the point of entry.
All right, she said with a coolness
that burned like ice on the tongue.
Take me but know that I shall die in your place.
What melodrama! I smiled and, her skin as soft as fur pelts,
I sank into her for what seemed hours.
After, we lay back dripping with sweat
to talk as true lovers will, of our most secret desires.
Well, I guess I spoke most of my need for her only her
like the singers often sing.
She smiled again and asked for my fan.
Surely you have not forgotten I shall die in your place.
Find me in Butoku Hall. She vanished
without even opening the door. Not a trace of her in the alley.
I ran to Butoku Hall. There on the floor
lay a bloody fox with a fan over its face.
Forever grateful every night I copy the Lotus Sutra
dedicating it to her memory, that in the figure I knew
she will rise to the heavens with wings like fans.

The Elements

My hair and clothes smell like shit,

my body is gray from the soot of other people's chimney smoke—

their broiled fish, rice, miso. What I would give

for a baked sweet potato.

Here I am for the townsfolk to scorn

as they walk to work or market:

the homeless woman who got what she deserved.

The nag. The thief.

The one who cut off the sparrow's tongue.

One moment I was having a bad day,

the next I was losing it,

chasing a bird with my shears

for eating rice starch.

History is not kind: not men's versions of conquest

or my own small history. Never

turning my back on my father or brothers,

never sleeping through a night

without pinches, pushes, and yes, being fucked

while my mother's ashes scattered further from my life.

For New Year's, a single orange,

maybe new straw boots. My doll

was made of scraps my mother had saved

after sewing other women's kimonos. She's here in my sleeve.

Yes. All these years I have protected her

from the elements.

The Snake

There are some things you can't help

when you're young or when you're asleep

try as you might.

I was a young acolyte visiting a compound with my master

and felt like sleeping away from the others

so chose an out-of-the-way corner.

There, in my dreams, a stunning woman

lifted my sex to her lips and drew me out of my body—

soul and liquid both.

Even before waking I knew it was a dream

but when I opened my eyes, to my horror I saw a dead snake

curled by my mat, its mouth glistening with semen.

I ran to the bath and scrubbed my body till it was sore.

What I really needed was to confide in someone

but I didn't want to be known as "the monk sucked off by a snake."

Eventually I did tell a friend

who merely warned me never to sleep in such forlorn spots.

Word did get around after all

which is why I'm telling you this myself.

The Old Woman's Breast

They say childbirth is painful.
I wouldn't know about that.
I do know it's painful without children.
To wait for nothing. Nothing
as river, horse, boat. I know
it's painful to wade through water
so cold the feet turn blue, the lips
blue and gravel bloodies the instep
even as the sand smoothes. I jumped in
to pull out the enormous fruit
I saw as I laundered our clothes.
I heard it—loop, lip-lip
loop, lip-lip, loop loop, lip—gurgling by
then catch in dead branches.
I slipped across currents until I reached the bank.
There I wiped my legs, arms
and this incredible peach in dirty laundry.
I warmed it in my lap,
smelling a sweet rusty scent
much like the river bed. The skin dried
fuzzy. My mouth watered.
As I picked up a blade to slice through
the orange and red
my gut trembled and throbbed so violently
I shouted tremendous shouts splitting open the flesh
and lay bare a small perfect child
with a round head, pink skin and tiny penis
that shot urine across the grass.
He opened his mouth to cry
and I cried also.
This would be our baby.
My calendar. My seasons.
I ate some peach, wrapped him in cotton cloth
and tucked him into my jacket.
He sucked on my withered breast and it filled so full
he choked on the milk. Imagine that.

THE HEMISPHERE: KUCHUK HANEM

> "Flaubert's encounter with an Egyptian
> courtesan produced a widely influential
> model of the Oriental woman.... He spoke
> for and represented her."
> [SAID, *ORIENTALISM*, P. 6]

I am four. It is a summer midafternoon, my nap finished. I cannot find
her. I hear the water in the bathroom. Not from the faucet but occasional
splashes. I hear something like the bar of soap fall in. I cannot find her.

Flaubert's encounter, Flaubert's encounter, Flaubert's encounter—

I stand outside the white door. Reflected in the brass knob I see my face
framed by a black pixie-cut. More splashes.

I hear humming. It is mother's voice in the bathroom through the closed
door and it is midafternoon. No light from beneath the door. I twist the
knob and hang my weight to pull it open. In the half-light I see mother
sitting in the bath: the white porcelain, gray, the yellow tiles, gray. Her
hair is coiled and pinned up.

I see her breasts above the edge of the tub. I have never seen my mother
without her clothes. Her nipples.

"[S]he never spoke of herself, she never represented her emotions,
presence, or history. [*Flaubert*] spoke for and represented her." [SAID, 6]

Her nipples appear dark and round. They are funny and beautiful. I
leave, perhaps to lie down on my pillow or find my bear. What did she
say to me? Did she scold? Laugh? Just smile or ignore me? My breasts
have never looked like those breasts.

"He was foreign, comparatively wealthy, male and these were historical facts of domination that allowed him not only to possess Kuchuk Hanem physically but to speak for her and tell his readers in what way she was 'typically Oriental.'" [SAID, 6]

In 1850 a woman with skin the color of sand in the shade of the Sphinx, midday, meant little and of course mine was seen more than veiled and I could earn a living "dancing." What I liked best were gifts of chocolate. Usually from a French man thinking I'd consider the evening amorous and reduce the rate. Paris must be lovely but for the French.

Maybe I want a penis. Maybe that's why I love sitting on an out-stretched man and, his prick between my legs, rubbing it as if it were mine. Maybe that's why I love to put a cock in my mouth, feel it increase in size with each stroke, each lick, each pulse. Taste the Red Sea. Look over or up and see the man barely able to contain himself, pulling on my nipples or burying a tongue into my Persian Gulf. Also barely able to contain my own sluice. Maybe it's my way to possess a cock. For a moment feel hegemonic and Western.

I have an addiction to silk and chocolate—gold a little. But coins are a necessity. Now chocolates—if there's a plate of chocolate I cannot stop my hand. I tell the Nubian to take it to the kitchen and store it in a cool place. I will sniff it out. Find her fingerprints on the sweaty sweets.

We both use our mouths, professionally.

> *"My heart begins to pound everytime I see [a prostitute] in low-cut dresses walking under the lamplight in the rain, just as monks in their corded robes have always excited some deep ascetic corner of my soul...."*

Maybe it's my way to possess a cock. For a moment feel hegemonic and Western.

"The idea of prostitution is a meeting of so many elements—lust, bitterness, complete absence of human contact, muscular frenzy, the clink of gold—that to peer into it deeply makes one reel. One learns so many things in a brothel, and feels such sadness, and dreams so longingly of love!" [FLAUBERT,10]

I watch white couples. See how they touch the clitoris. A cat lapping, a cat pawing. Think about betrayal and loss.

The two girls invited their cousin Conrad in the little pool, to see his small penis wobbling about like a party favor.

Playing with the costume jewelry in her mother's drawers then hiding under her vanity, the bathroom door opened, steam poured out and she saw her father naked from the waist down. Swollen balls. Penis dangling. A raw red.

It's true when all is said and done, I am less a dancer than a whore. Men pay me money, stick their cocks in me, laugh, weep, curse, or silently ride my body. And leave. That's what I am, a whore and alone. To be despised by the men because who else would let them come as they come but someone with vagrant morals. Despised by wives, mistresses, and fiancées for my abilities, independence, the peculiar attention that I receive. I am scorned by the religious. By the courts and by my parents. But I do not fear a man's departure. Know that.

And I have made a name for myself that will, Flaubert boasts on his own behalf, not mine, that will cover the globe. Know that. That the image is not my own. My image does not entirely belong to me. And neither does yours, master or slave.

When he writes about Egypt he will write what he has experienced: the adoration of the historical Cleopatra from boyhood lessons, Kuchuk

*Hanem—my cunt, my dance—the Nile, the squalor, a man slitting his belly
and pulling his intestines in and out then bandaging himself with cotton and
oils, people fucking animals which I'm told also happens in France but not in
the cities. Because there are no animals.*

I knew what he wanted. He wanted to fuck me. He guessed I was 16,
his sister's age when he last saw her at Christmas while she knelt at
Mass, candles lighting her profile. But I was 13. I wore ankle bracelets
from Indian shops. Earrings that jingled in the breeze. And a bikini so
small I would never wear it before my father. Why would this
Portuguese sailor come over to me and in his broken English point to
the tatoo of a geisha as if I would identify with it. And I did a little.

He wanted someone who did not resemble his mother or his friends'
sisters or wives. The mistress he had dumped before departure. He wanted
license. The kind available not even in one's own imagination—but in
geographic departure.

> *"The morning we arrived in Egypt...we had scarcely set foot on shore
> when Max, the old lecher, got excited over a negress who was drawing
> water at a fountain. He is just as excited by the little negro boys. By
> whom is he not excited? Or, rather, by* what?" [FLAUBERT, 43]

He will think that I am one thing, even as he learns about me. He will
believe those things and make them true even while he remembers my
eyes, organs no different from his own. Yet what he witnesses on tour
and what I see daily are experienced differently. Does no one bugger
animals in France? Does no one martyr himself? It is why he adores
prostitutes and monks. Adores.

Mother has removed the dish rack and all the dishes, sponges and
cleansers from the kitchen sink. She places an old blue towel to the side
and fills the basin a little. With one hand she props up the baby who

teethes on the faucet. With the other she swirls soap in little circles all over her head and body then pours water over her. The baby looks surprised and angry. She opens her red mouth and cries. She will smell good, like powder, not pee and sour milk, when she falls asleep on the carpet. Mother will read to me.

The air smells of garlic.

I have become a continent.

He liked to fart under a cover then plunge under to smell the gas. I laughed but it wasn't really funny. Moreover I do not assume all French relish that activity.

A French man who never traveled here, which is to say, never made my acquaintance, wrote a poem about me, Kuchuk Hanem, based on letters written to him by Flaubert. It made Flaubert's mistress, his former mistress, furious. It amuses but does not please me.

> *"This is a great place for contrasts: splendid things gleam in the dust. I performed on a mat that a family of cats had to be shooed off—a strange coitus, looking at each other without being able to exchange a word, and the exchange of looks is all the deeper for the curiosity and surprise. My brain was too stimulated for me to enjoy it much otherwise. These shaved cunts make a strange effect—the flesh is as hard as bronze, and my girl had a splendid arse."* [FLAUBERT, 44]

I have become a continent. I have become half the globe.

She will read from Grimm's Fairy Tales where the youngest daughter is always the prettiest and the stepmother murderous. Her hands smell of garlic from our dinner.

A hemisphere.

After our last hour outside, riding bikes or the tire swing, my sister and I bathe the mud off then slip between white sheets. 1961. The sheets are always white.

> *"Kuchuk Hanem is a tall, splendid creature, lighter in coloring than an Arab...slightly coffee-colored. When she bends, her flesh ripples into bronze ridges...her black hair, wavy, unruly, pulled straight back on each side from a center parting beginning at the forehead; small braids joined together at the nape of the neck. She has one upper incisor, right, which is beginning to go bad."* [FLAUBERT, 114]

What she wanted was to sit on her mother's lap and be small. Smaller than her mother and smaller than her mother's lap. She wanted not to realize the breadth of separation that arrives with growing up, gradual, never complete: crawling, playing hide-and-seek...sneaking a cigarette...a neon-yellow bikini.

With the other hand she swirls soap around in little circles all over her head and body then pours water over her. The baby looks surprised and angry.

curry stains under mother's cuticles—

> *"She asks us if we would like a little entertainment, but Max says that first he would like to entertain himself alone with her, and they go downstairs. After he finished, I go down and follow his example. Groundfloor room, with a divan and a cafas [basket] with a mattress."* [FLAUBERT, 115]

The hotel salon made an error and not only trimmed my bangs but curled my hair. For a ten-year-old this excited and threatened. In a bus I feared people might think I was with my father, a sexual companion, because I do not resemble him unless you look closely: short knobby fingers, high bridge, gray rings beneath my eyes. Red highlights in my jet hair.

A Chinese American man, manager of a clothing chainstore, was astonished by my daughter's beauty. He could not take his eyes off her as she increased her antics around the shop mirrors: rock star, beauty pageant queen, Olympic gymnast. He could not believe a Eurasian mix could produce such a creature. Blue-eyed like an animal. Against dominant genes.

a hemisphere

The female body as imperialists colony is not a new symbol. Sexual impulse as revolutionary impulse? Do women depend upon the sexual metaphor for identity, an ironic figure of speech? Will I fall into the trap of writing from the imperialists' point of view? From a patriarchal one? How can we write erotica and not? What would an anti-imperialistic framework look like? Are not women the original keepers of narrative? Of lineage?

"For Egypt was not just another colony: it was the vindication of Western imperialism; it was, until its annexation by England, an almost academic example of Oriental backwardness; it was to become the triumph of English knowledge and power." [SAID, 35]

What does a national liberation movement contain for women? Does liberation encompass history, expression, memory? Can it nurture?

Can I speak for her? For the Turkish, Nubian, the—brown, black, blacker?

The women were in competition for men. For silk, cosmetics, fresh dates, survival. Dowries, a pale fantasy.

> *"Kuchuk's dance is brutal. She squeezes her bare breasts together with her jacket. She puts on a girdle fashioned from a brown shawl with gold stripes, with three tassels hanging on ribbons...."* [FLAUBERT, 115]

What is contained in the brutality?

If he had loved her enough, needed her in his bones enough, would he have brought her home? Could he hurt his mother, his friends, his former lovers, his career? With a black whore? Even such a famous one?

If you are dependent on prostitutes, write about them, dream about them, masturbate dreaming about them—can you pretend objectivity? Can you kiss your mother or sister without twitching?

> *"Kuchuk dances the Bee...[shedding] her clothing as she danced. Finally she was naked except for a fichu which she held in her hands and behind which she pretended to hide, and at the end she threw down the fichu. That was the Bee. She danced it very briefly and said she does not like to dance that dance."* [FLAUBERT, 117]

> *"Coup with Safia Zugairah—I stain the divan. She is very corrupt and writhing, extremely voluptuous. But the best was the second copulation with Kuchuk. Effect of her necklace between my teeth. Her cunt felt like rolls of velvet as she made me come."* [FLAUBERT, 117]

Her name, talents, and shaved cunt have outlived her person. We remember her for the dance and the fuck. For the hemisphere created. But what would she have said? Could the words be translated?

What did she say to Gustave or Max?

The way I wish mother to speak up so I can become a woman.

The way I trespass the boundaries of fiction and non-fiction.

The way nothing is ever verbatim.

> "We went to bed; she insisted on keeping the outside. Lamp: the wick
> rested in an oval cup with a lip; after some violent play, coup. She falls
> asleep with her hand in mine. She snores. The lamp, shining feebly, cast
> a triangular gleam, the color of pale metal, on her beautiful forehead;
> the rest of her face was in shadow. Her little dog slept on my silk
> jacket.... I dozed off with my fingers passed through her necklace, as
> though to hold her should she awake.... At quarter of three, we wake—
> another coup, this time very affectionate.... I smoke a sheesheh...."
> **[FLAUBERT, 118–9]**

> "She snores." **[IBID.]**

What is the context? Who hears and records the material?

If you use a language where the subject comes first, where je comes first,
can you even pretend objectivity?

Of course there was no agreement: Flaubert fucked her and wrote about
her. His words. His worlds.

She opened her red mouth and cried.

Am I seeking an older sister to care for me: show me how to wax my
legs, manicure my nails, henna my hair. Walk in stilettos.

To call me a woman.

To teach children a language not to listen and obey, but to engage in narratives.

Is it the story or the story of the story?

> *"We have not yet seen any dancing girls; they are all in exile in Upper Egypt. Good brothels no longer exist in Cairo, either.... But we have seen male dancers."* [FLAUBERT, 83]

Cannot subvert a category without being engaged.

> *"A week ago I saw a monkey in the street jump on a donkey and try to jack him off—the donkey brayed and kicked.... [The secretary at the consulate] told me of having seen an ostrich trying to violate a donkey. Max had himself jacked off the other day in a deserted section among some ruins and said it was very good."* [FLAUBERT, 85-6]

Three wars have taught military men "about" Asian women. Orientals. Extended by the classifieds.

> *"We are leading a good life, my dear old darling [Mother]. Oh, how sorry I am that you are not here. How you would love it! If you knew what calm surrounds us, and how peaceful are the depths we feel our minds explore—we laze, we loaf, we daydream...."* [FLAUBERT, 105]

I hear her pour coffee. Open the refrigerator for milk. Walk without shoes to the living room. To a stack of magazines with cakes on the covers.

I hear her pour two cups of coffee.

I am four. It is summer midafternoon, my nap finished. I cannot find her. I hear the water splash in the bathroom. Not from the faucet but

occasional splashes. I hear something like the bar of soap fall in. I
cannot find her.

I hear her chopping vegetables.

Girls actually fainted. Dozens fell on the tarmac.

The first time I heard of the Beatles I was in third grade, leaning out
the police station window on the the second floor after baton-twirling
class. Christine Van Pelt leaned out with me and told me the Beatles
had landed at Idlewild Airport and girls had fainted. I told her I knew
though I didn't. Her family moved when she was ten. I heard from an
unreliable source that she quit high school and became a prostitute in
Boston. I can picture a young woman's large-boned body, full breasted.
Black corset and stockings. Blue eyes. What took her to that room?
That first john? Was it in part the way she and Mary Jo Murphey, who
lived above her Dad's auto parts garage, taunted me because I cried
easily? Or was it the way Christine slipped on my mother's tiny wedding
slippers, fitting her eight-year-old foot perfectly?

I remember him not for the sex but for the cool shower we took after
3 am. Holding and twisting each other under the hard spray, laughing at
the cold. We powder under the fan before I gently push him to the door.
To go home. To his wife. If he has one.

I am so hungry. I consume Said's text.

My questions strike a different facet: what does Desire seek? It must
become a radical question.

*The men want me, Flaubert wanted me, not for the sex but for the
experience...and especially the sadness he recovers in departure. He knows
he will not return once he leaves Esna for Turkey. But I know he will return*

(that's why he came in the first place, to never leave) perhaps in the sound of rain, invisible in the night. It may not snow in Esna but I know it rains in Paris.

Or the garlic she sliced.

I never receive enough attention. Never. I am jealous of every person, act, article. Is this my inheritance?

What does Desire desire? To be needed absolutely? To fill the other's life not just as a lover but as a mother—symbiotically? To be left alone?

"I thought of my nights in Paris brothels...." [FLAUBERT, 130]

Or the garlic she sliced.

A black girl from the neighborhood wore a t-shirt inscribed: Jewish girls don't swallow. Later I thought, I don't like to either.

Sam wanted to come in my mouth and, if not swallow, transfer it to his. The idea lovely, the reality less appetizing. A real romantic. The best features of that affair: his Rambler's front seat, his cooking with eggplants, his phone messages, his stories about learning to swim which needed to be written down to overcome his writer's block.

She learned to swim in a mossy lake, the fish bumping her ankles like dust. The algae in her hair. A harmless snake by the beach.

A man outside the Love Pharmacy, longish hair pinned back, picked red nail polish off his finger absent-mindedly.

My mother shopped for a bikini with me and I couldn't believe she approved of a very small yellow one that fastened in the front. I could pass for 15. I felt embarrassed showing the bikini to my father. He taught at the Art Institute that summer. From our hotel room I could see over the Lake—see storm clouds floating toward us, lightning beating inside. The dark rain flicking down sharp as razors. I loved Chicago.

My nap is finished. I hear water in the bathroom. Not from the faucet but occasional splashes. I hear something like the bar of soap fall in. I am four.

My sister and I go to the beach by ourselves. I brought a transistor to connect myself to the rest of the world. One afternoon as I lay on my towel a wiry tanned man in a small aqua bathing suit walked over and asked to sit beside me. He did not speak much English but conveyed that he was a sailor from Portugal. Swarthy. In hindsight probably mid-20s. By way of conversation he pointed to a large tattoo on his arm; an intricately designed geisha after Utamaro. He smiled as if somehow I identified with this. I did a little. He asked if I'd like to board his ship.

In Chicago my knowledge of sex increased rapidly: the call asking if I'd like to model for *Seventeen*...what color my hair, eyes...nipples? pink or brown?...did I know what oral sex was? what? I told the man I couldn't say because my parents were in the room. My father grabbed the phone. I felt like vomiting.

The evening my sister and I ate at Taco Villas' I forgot the money and ran back to the hotel. Around the corner I ran past a man rubbing his protruding cock. Another time a man sitting on a bus, his cock sticking out of his shorts, covered and exposed it with his hat. Pitiful belongings.

Chateaubriand inscribed his name on the Pyramids. [SAID, 175]

The two little girls hold a truce as they abandon Barbies and climb into the tub, giggling as the water rises from their body weight. They hug. They sit on each other's laps. They lay across each other's soapy bodies, gray bubbles ringing the porcelain. Reveal to the other her "penis."

Two cups of coffee.

Even after washing my hands for dinner, after rinsing the dishes—

She could not wash off her patrons but she could wash off their sweat, saliva, cum. The ring of dirt around her neck. The kohl they loved to smear as if blackening her eye. Pour a cup of coffee. Sometimes she felt scattered. Sometimes collected. She wished she could visit her sister.

What would Kuchuk Hanem say if I were to sit beside her in the predawn, tobacco wafting into our hair like the memory of my first husband studying for exams. The fragrance of a coffee as rich as the mud from the Nile that must flood the fields to award farmers a relatively easy season, or predict irrigating with buckets haled from the same, circa 1840. The thick silt coating the land, the throat, the tongue. Sheer caffeine heightening the blue tiles as we turn towards one another. Would she have offered to put on her veil and go out herself to the market for figs or ask her slave to fetch some.

If you are forbidden to dance it's all you want. You might make love instead, you might eat—but it's all to dance. And it's a dance that makes the travelers open their eyes as one does in climax or terror, taste the sea fill the mouth till he swallows it back, and the heart's wings beat bloody, a bird caged in the market, though our Koran prescribes a proper slaughter.

Would she offer me figs and ask me to stay or tell me to get the hell out, what's a married woman doing here—curious? You want lessons? You want me? You looking for someone? It must mean something that our hearts are cut by men like a dress pattern, but sewn by women.

Show me your clitoris.

Do I seek an older sister?

I cannot find her. I hear the water in the bathroom. Occasional splashes. I hear something like the bar of soap fall in.

I hear her chopping vegetables.

They did not know, or maybe could not desecrate "mother's" tit, did not know nipples can glow like the clitoris.

Who is the cartographer? Male or female?

Under what circumstances does a person have choice? Under what circumstances does a woman?

"When it was time to leave I didn't leave...I sucked her furiously—her body was covered with sweat—she was tired after dancing—she was cold...."

The light in Egypt reminded her of the moon—black shade and white sunlight.

"I covered her with my pelisse, and she fell asleep with her fingers in mine. As for me, I scarcely shut my eyes. Watching that beautiful creature asleep (she snored, her head against my arm: I had slipped my forefinger under her necklace), my night was one long, infinitely intense reverie—that was why I stayed. I thought of my nights...."

She "looked like" a lesbian only because she conveyed a sense of not putting up with shit.

> *"...in Paris brothels—a whole series of memories came back—and I thought of her, of her dance, of her voice as she sang songs that for me were without meaning and even without distinguishable words."*
> [FLAUBERT, 130]

The need to belong overwhelms—to hold my own sister, hold her hand or link arms. Rest a cheek against her neck. To feel in my daughter, my sister. To feel in my mother, my sister. To feel in my sister, my self.

"You know you want it and it's big"..."Sit on my face, China"..."Nice titties"..."Do you want me to teach you some English?"..."Are you from Saigon?"

What is my stake in this?

Woman's role as storyteller included creator and healer. My mother knew this, unconsciously.

After I cook garlic, chop it, dice it, sliver it up, spread it over the crackling oil, I can smell it on my fingers even after I have washed my hands for dinner. Even while I am eating the pasta. Even after eating chocolates.

> *"[Dear Louise,] The oriental woman is no more than a machine: she makes no distinction between one man and another man. Smoking, going to the baths, painting her eyelids and drinking coffee—such is the circle of occupations within which...."*

Even after having washed the children. Even after drinking coffee and throwing out the grounds. Even after cutting my finger on the dog food can. Sucking it. Bandaging my finger. Showering outdoors in the twilight.

> *"...within which her existence is confined. As for physical pleasure, it must be very slight, since the well known button, the seat of same, is sliced off at an early age...."*

Even after television and a bowl of popcorn. After washing the dishes in hot sudsy water. After reading Said's *Orientalism*. After touching every crease and crevice of my husband's body.

> *"...is sliced off at an early age.... You tell me that Kuchuk's bedbugs degrade her in your eyes; for me they were the most enchanting touch of all. Their nauseating odor mingled with the scent of her skin which was dripping with sandalwood oil...."* [FLAUBERT, 220]

Even after drifting into sleep my fingers smell of the garlic I sliced for dinner.

> *"[Dear Louis,] At Esna I saw Kuchuk Hanem again; it was sad. I found her changed. She had been sick. I shot my bolt with her only once."*
> [FLAUBERT, 200]

Even after drifting into sleep my fingers smell of the garlic I sliced for dinner. I am hungry when I wake to the baby's cries at 2 am. My breasts are leaking as well. The milk may also taste of garlic. I drink a glass of water.

I hear a starling stuck in the chimney.

Father sets up a pink and blue folding bassinet, a tube running in to the bathtub. Mother places my sister into the tepid water. Uses a square, white soap.

We powder by the window before I gently push him to the door. To go home under the stars that vanish if you stare for very long.

No light from beneath the door.

My bad tooth aches.

My mother might have told me this story but she died suddenly a few months ago.

THE STORY AND THE DAUGHTERS

Every story began with the same words,
mukashi mukashi aruhi,
and although you did not understand exactly
you knew this was how stories began
and the big pictures translated the rest
as if you were a baby realizing sounds as sounds
that had to be sorted and resorted.

Recollecting the stories mother read to you
you try to locate one that might have prepared you
for loss, a child's loss, even a grown child's loss
of his or her mother. But among the peaches,
foxes, teapots, not one
comforts or echoes what one seeks
when the mother is struck by a car,
killed instantly, before she could open her eyes
and think *something is wrong,*
my chest is broken, my heart crushed, before she
wondered, *where is my breath?*

There is the one of a childless bamboo cutter
who finds a little girl inside a glowing stalk
and carries her home to his wife. You can't
recall her name, something-*hime* probably.
And because your sister is completing field work
for her dissertation you can't reach her to ask.
And father wouldn't know. But the name is essential
and may have a moon reference because
at the end of the story she returns to the moon
having given the couple the pleasure of raising
a perfect child and she, the honor
of serving them in many ordinary ways: serving tea,
rubbing their backs, singing with forest animals.

But you don't want this story to be the story

to prepare you for loss because you have your own daughters.
You want a story about a mother who is lifted by a cloud
or rides the back of an ancient tortoise
and waves goodbye to the remaining villagers.
To say goodbye. How to say goodbye to a mother
forever is something father realized we do not learn.
And you do blame her a little
for not finding a story if there is a story
with giant pictures, onomatopoeic phrases, curious names.
She might have shown us how to endure her loss
just as she taught my daughters the names of fruits:
momo, ringo, orenji, banana.
To avoid the number four, a homonym for death,
and to never pass food from your chopsticks
to someone else's, like bones at a cremation.
And now you remember her name is Kaguyahime
but must look for a dictionary because
she is not here to tell you what it means.
Still because she did not leave a story to salve loss
you must use the elements she did give you (magic,
courage, foreshadowing...) to construct one for yourself
and your children who have tried to locate
their own small explanations:

Mukashi mukashi aruhi two little girls
decided to visit their sick grandmother and grandfather
who lived on a nearby island. The oldest, Miya,
was just the age to cut through the bamboo grove
and cross the bay to reach their farm.
The youngest, Rei, gathered potatoes and onions for soup.
The father gave them coins for the ferry
and the two set off along a winding path
where the light splintered across their faces
and quilted jackets. Rei was wearing too-big socks
and kept pausing to pull them up.

Miya's hair kept tangling in branches
until she tied it back. Near the last bend
they found a baby sparrow who had fallen from its nest
and was still with death. They buried it beside a stone wall
then dusted off their hands. From the dense bamboo grove
hundreds of small animals peeked out.
At the shore the ferry captain told them to board
with four other passengers: a farmer, circus performer,
teacher and doctor. The girls sat at the bow,
the wind blasting their faces till the salt stung their eyes
and they retreated below to eat rice balls. Everything tasted
like the sea. They smiled at each other.
This was only the fourth trip they'd traveled alone!
Upon disembarking they noticed two people in the distance
waving wildly. Why and how did their parents get here so fast!
"Mother, Father—" they began.
Their mother choked on tears
when she tried to speak. They felt their hearts beating
all through their bodies even in their palms and teeth.
"Girls, come sit on this sunny bench," their father said.
He hugged them. He felt sweaty. They were quiet
and did not even hear the other passengers
greeted by their own families.
Finally Miya and her mother walked to the dock together
and she told her the terrible news from the chrysanthemum farm:
"Grandma's fever soared last night and she died
even before the sun rose." Miya cried quietly
until she was out of breath.
Her grandmother had often taken care of her
especially when she had scarlet fever.
She looked forward to returning her care.
But the first thing she asked was,
"Will Grandpa find a new wife to be our Grandmother?"
Her mother's raised eyebrows relaxed
as she realized Miya momentarily
searched beyond her loss.

She held her and they cried openly
until their bodies shook.
The father had told Rei separately
to allow her her own response. She said to him,
"That's strange. I was sick and didn't die."
So he explained how every creature
grows old and weaker, less able to fight a fever.
"Where is Grandma now?"
"She is part of the air, wind, sun and shadow
around us," he answered.
After scowling hard she asked:
"When we take the ferry will she come home with us?
When we breathe will she become a part of us?
When we are sick will she still take care of us?"
Rei had a hundred questions and kept asking them all week.
They and their aunts, uncles and cousins
cared for grandpa until his fever was down
and he could manage with just an older granddaughter.
Then the two girls and their parents boarded the ferry.
They sat at the bow and as the belts of wind
blew back their hair and clothes they called out,
"Grandma, Grandma, Grandma" till their throats hurt.
In the midst of their shouting
hundreds of golden fish leapt from the waves
and ahead of the ferry the forest animals
gathered at the water to lead them home.
Miya tossed the remaining rice to them.
Rei asked if the universe was larger
now that grandma lived inside it.

When you finally read this story to your daughters
they ask you to tell it to them again. Please.

NOTES

THE FLOODING and WISTERIA

References to Genji and other characters are from the Japanese classic, *The Tale of Genji*, by Murasaki Shikibu. "Wisteria" refers in part to the "fuji" in Genji's stepmother's name, Fujitsubo.

CRUISING BARTHES

The quotations with page numbers are from Roland Barthes' *The Pleasure of the Text*, translated by Richard Miller; the other quotations are from *Life* magazine as indicated. (E. Barnes, "Lost Boys of the Sudan," *Life*, June 1992, pp. 50–58.)

THE HEMISPHERE: KUCHUK HANEM

Indented sections are from *Flaubert in Egypt*, translated and edited by Francis Steegmuller (Copyright ©1972 by Francis Steegmuller. Reprinted by permission of McIntosh and Otis, Inc.). Edward Said quotations are from his book *Orientalism* (Copyright ©1978 by Edward W. Said. Reprinted by permission of Pantheon Books).

KIMIKO HAHN was born outside New York City in 1955 to two art the late Maude Miyako Hamai from Hawai'i and Walter Hahn fr Wisconsin. Her previous books are the poetry collections *Air Pocke Earshot*, and *We Stand Our Ground* (with Susan Sherman and Gale Jackson). She has received fellowships from the National Endowment for the Arts and the New York Foundation for the Arts. In 1995, she was granted the Theodore Roethke Poetry Award for *Earshot*. A professor of poetry writing and literature at Queens College/CUNY, Hahn lives in Brooklyn with her husband, Ted Hannan, and their daughters, Miyako Tess and Reiko Lily.

sts,
m